THINKING MY WAY TO THE TOP

Dr. Adrian Singleton

Table of Contents

DEDICATION

This book is dedicated to those who have trusted, motivated, and encouraged me. In addition, they have also allowed me to lead and protect their lives. That is my family.

To my wife, Crystal, your passion for my success has always been my energy. Thank you for listening to my countless dreams and ideas for 20 years. Your encouragement has always been my fuel to keep pushing.

Marquet, Arianna & Christian Singleton. Thank you for not only allowing me to live my dreams but to live them with you.

I also want to thank my parents, Horace and Linda Jackson, for your consistent encouragement in my life.

I would like to thank my Mother and Father in Love, Dennis and Sallie Greenleaf, for your consistent support over the last 20 years.

All of my siblings, much love for your respect and support.

I also have to acknowledge those that have pushed me to write my first book, Drs. Martin and Lynnell Williams. I am so motivated by your leadership and commitment to impacting the World.

Last but not least, I have to send my gratitude to the late Dr. Myles Munroe and Pastor Ruth Munroe. Thank you for always accepting me as a mentee and a son and for believing in my dreams. Your dedication to my excellence will never be forgotten.

INTRODUCTION

As I was driving through the Houston traffic one day, I was wondering about all the reasons that the people around me and I were in that traffic. There were so many cars, and I thought if I did not have to be here, I would not, and I assumed the same about everyone else. I realized that everyone in that traffic was there for one particular goal – the same goal. And that goal specifically is success. Everyone wants to be successful for their family.

Some simply have an idea: they want to be successful. Some have received training to help them succeed; some pray for the opportunity to grow every day; some have optimistic mindsets and they think they will simply get favor for that particular day (which you can have). Some heard an encouraging message maybe from a church or a mosque, or somewhere else and they bought into some kind of optimistic idea that they can go into the workplace and be successful. Some people are just happy to have a job but feel they will be stuck in the same position for the next 20 years based on the generational mindset of the family they are from.

Regardless of the above categories a person may fall in, this book is about helping people see that there is a higher calling on their life than what they are experiencing right now. In this book, I want to share strategic secrets of the marketplace including entering the marketplace, understanding the language of the marketplace, developing relationships in the marketplace, and developing favor in the marketplace. It begins with favor which is uncommon influence and power that can be used with character or, shall I say, gained favor through reciprocity.

I have been in the business industry for nearly 20 years, and in my career what I have learned is that people are people. They all think differently, create differently, and have different ideals in life. Some people are bothered by the fact we are all different, but there is power when you get various mindsets in a room and lead them in one direction. Everyone there is **right**, but everyone is right in the **wrong** direction. The question is how can you turn all of those rights in one direction?

Because as you are driving these ideas to one direction, you may find you have a lot of strong personalities in the room. Over the years, I have worked with many different people: CEOs, CFOs, Executive Vice Presidents, Directors, Managers, Supervisors, and other employees. I have worked with the people who ran the company and the people that cleaned the bathrooms.

I have worked in many different types of arenas. I have worked with all sorts of people: those that have power, those that have influence, those that have character, those that have power with no influence, those that have power with influence, those that have power with character, those that have power with no character, those that have influence with character, etc.

The talent my Creator has given me is to work with all types of people and lead all their ideas in one direction. The reality of what we are experiencing today is that we are dealing with all different types of personalities. Just think, as you drive down the road, how many new ideas are coming to mind for many people, but they do not know how to capitalize on those ideas? How many professors have seen potential in students, but they do not know how to foster those potential talents into reality?

How many of you have been in a system: for example, a business, and you have noticed that in that system, some people thrive, and some do not? Some rise to the top of the class and some are average.

This book is about giving you the tools of wisdom and understanding, to help you gain the success you want in the marketplace.

My motivation in writing this book is this: I have noticed over the years that when I visit church services, when I sit with people, everyone in those services goes back to a work industry that he/she does not have the tools or the understanding to consistently move themselves up to a level of high potential influence.

Throughout my journey, I have used this tool to become a high influencer in any and every arena because I have made the progression of really understanding people.

There are certain ways to understand different personalities, and I have taken the time to become an expert in the social skills, and an expert in the disc personality test because I know that people think, react, walk and smell (yes, I said smell) differently in their lives.

So how do we focus all these ideas and personalities together? What is the chemistry behind making all of these ideas come to life with people? What is the chemistry behind a person's body language when he says no, but he really means yes? What is the chemistry behind a person's body language when he wants to say yes, but he is not in the position to say yes, so he has to give you a no? What happens when you are asking for an opportunity and the person says no because he does not have the power to say yes?

What gives you the ability to go inside this arena to know that you can create and turn every no into a yes, even if their no was a no?

As we dig deep into this book, I will give you strategies and understandings of historical points of some of the greatest writers in the world that I have tested myself. I have become a student of many of these great techniques and I have proven for almost 20 years that they can work. I cannot say that I have done all of them by myself. I have had great mentors, great teachers, fathers, mothers, and friends. My biological parents have been great influences in my life. My wife, especially, has really been the quiet storm of wisdom and the whisperer in my ear to help me see that these strategies work, even in our marriage and family. These tools will give your children the ability to come out from the school and enter the system to be world leaders.

I have traveled afar to Mexico, the UK, China, South Korea & Canada proving these techniques. What is quite interesting to me is that many of the people I have met abroad are motivated to create an opportunity for their children to come to America to gain influence and they have been very successful at doing so. You may ask how does he know this? I am glad you asked. It is because I have befriended many of them. And I have become close to their families because I believe every person that pumps blood in their body has the ability to be successful.

Whether we accept it or not, we all are a part of the marketplace. This book strategically talks about how to influence the marketplace and how to take your ideas out of your mind and make them a reality inside the marketplace.

CHAPTER 1:
LEADERSHIP

As we talk about influence in the marketplace, we have to talk about leadership. We have to discuss how and why you should find your own personal leadership. We have to talk about specializing in your own personal leadership and what that all entails. We have to discuss who your mentors are, the people you allow to speak into your life, and what type of education you need to entangle yourself in. If you are going to impact the marketplace, you cannot do it without leadership.

A large component of leadership is influence: how to influence people outside of your comfort zone by discovering their hidden personalities (without requesting them to take a test). In many situations, companies or individuals require people to take a test so we can understand how their personalities are built.

But what if you studied people to understand their actions so you could easily identify their personality skills before you even have a conversation with them? You would know how they would react, what their body language says and how you react to them. Believe it or not, there are techniques that can help you understand people's body language and how you can relate to them once you understand their personality. You can simply look into someone's eyes and understand that everyone has a different level of personality.

These tools are the things we use every day to help us understand the magnitude of who we are. Once you understand how to connect with individuals based on their personality, every human becomes simple to connect with.

How to Choose the Right Mentorship

Sometimes, at first glance, the world looks so big. But the following story reminds me of how to easily identify the world when it comes down to influence in the marketplace.

Many times in life, we have to decide whether to be on the good side or the bad side, the right or the wrong. The same thing happens in the marketplace, what side do you want to be on? We can decide to be a part of the good or decide to be a part of the bad.

This story is about a man, I will call him Mike. Mike had the opportunity to decide what side he wanted to be on. Mike was promised access to every part of the marketplace if he agreed to Sam's mentorship. Mike realized that if he submitted to Sam's mentorship, he was going to owe everything he accomplished to Sam. There were going to be a lot of strings attached.

What Mike did not realize was that his father had already worked hard to give him access to everything in the marketplace – access to own all of it. He would have the opportunity to go into any field, any location and still be successful. He just had to go down the right path of sharpening his skills by choosing the right school, the right mentor, the right people to follow, in order to be successful in his environment.

Sam may have really wanted to help Mike, but Sam had a track record of not being loyal, and not being consistent. Mike knew that if he submitted to Sam's mentorship, he would end up in the same boat as those before him. He decided to choose that life not knowing that his father had already taken care of these situations, that all he needed to do was just to take the right path in order to get there.

Sometimes in life, we have to decide if we are going to submit our lives to certain individuals. They may be great leaders, they may have great names, and be experts in their fields. I have found that some people may want to help you, but they simply cannot.

That is how I look at the world. I see that we have several opportunities in the marketplace, whether you want to go into media, business, religion, education, medicine, entertainment, law, etc. These are all various arenas in the marketplace.

These arenas push you to make some decisions — what you will specialize in, the right school to go to, the most ideal people you can connect to, the certifications you need to be recognized in that area, and the mentors you should submit your life to so that you can be recognized.

The challenge is: how do you choose the right ones? Here are some questions to ask:

1. Are they someone **you** respect in this arena?
2. Are they transparent in relation to their wins as equally as to their losses?
3. Are they well respected in the arena?

Characteristics of a Mentor

Many people do not want to think about the word "submission". There are so many people that have been exactly where you are: striving to be in the business arena. Just as it is said, "there's nothing new under the sun". As you are specializing in certain areas, you will find that mentorship is vitally important. How can a mentor help you?

- A mentor can help you because he can give you something in five minutes that took him 30 years to get. Like an athlete, he practices daily for his competition. He practices so he can quickly apply what he has learned from his coach and teammates on the field.

- A mentor will never be intimidated by your talent but will push you to be better than him.

- A mentor will open doors for you to simply walk through that took him years to enter.

The world looks so big, but in essence the world is so small. The marketplace level is the level everyone should understand, so that when they get there, they will be able to know how to sustain, be successful and be the expert in their field.

The next question is: Who are your teammates? How do you identify the right teammates to work with? How do the individuals you chose feel that they should be committed to your team? For me, my wife and children are my teammates. Their commitment to being a part of my dream happened because of a powerful word and that word is "reciprocity".

What is Reciprocity?

My first step was to truly value the people in my life and authentically want to invest in them. My family, friends and co-workers are excited to work with me and support my ideas simply because I valued their ideas **first**. Reciprocity may seem simple: what I do for you, you can do for me. But the culture of this word can open doors of opportunities with your name on them.

A huge collection of evidence showcases that reciprocity is a strong determinant of human behavior. One theory states that reciprocity is a social norm that includes exchanges between people, in a similar way, responding to another's action with another equal action. It is normally positive (returning a favor) but can be negative as well (punishment for a bad action).

At the heart of reciprocal exchange is the concept of giving, which can be used for benevolent reasons. For example, gifts may be utilized to sustain existing relationships or to make new ones. Gifts may be used to eliminate tension and to increase favor with a person that commonly disagrees with your agenda. Givers often acquire prestige and position in this way. Gifts may also be used to hold people liable for things so that one can keep them in line and require their loyalty. Another research theory shows that there are strings tied to giving that influence how people and groups associate with each other.

In the Indian tradition of gift presentation, it is more casual. It is believed that presents must be offered freely without any strings attached. In other communities, gift giving is a string between friends, a way of growing good relationships. In still other places, it has grown into an expensive, elaborate, and antagonistic ritual projected to mortify rivals by lavishing them with money and obligating them to reciprocate more in return.

Actually, the dichotomy among the two traditions of gift giving is more rhetorical and less behavioral; our generosity is not as unconditional as it appears. Organizations often apply the reciprocity culture in practice. It is used as a tool for social tempting in the form of "reciprocal concessions", which is believed to be an approach that involves a reasoning strategy. Reciprocal concessions are not bound to complications or critical decisions.

Reciprocal concessions can assist in improving outcome value, decision accuracy, and assess judgment. In some situations, groups are less influential when their members reject social influence. This type of influence can weaken group diversity directing to calamitous phenomena such as zealotry, rich-get-richer dynamics, and market bubble.

Humans are naturally inclined to reciprocate in social interaction. We respond to hostility with hostility and to respect with respect. Smiling staff receive more tips and violators are punished. We can say that social influence is mulled over through social interaction, and because of that, one may be curious if reciprocity expands to social influence itself.

Despite huge research on reciprocal behavior, to my knowledge, I have found no survey that has observed and reported the effect of reciprocity on how we influence others.

People can incorporate influential information from themselves and others on the basis of their confidence. Influential research on positioning oneself proposes strong evidence. The prediction made from this informational account is that social impact should hinge on the authenticity of the source and quality of advice, not on norms and conventions such as reciprocity.

Reciprocity in social psychology pertains to reacting to a positive act with another positive act, repaying kind actions. As a social concept, reciprocity means that people are much nicer and accommodating when treated with friendly actions than by the self-interest model. Conversely, as a response to hostile actions, people often react more brutally and nastier. In simple words, do something good, and people will feel urged to do something good for you in return.

We all understand how that feels. It is natural to all human beings to want to reciprocate like-treatments. If someone made us feel special in a certain way, we want to do something that causes them to feel the same. If they treat us good, we must do the same. If they mistreat us, we feel like throwing something negative at them. You cannot negate the feeling, but you surely can learn to point the triggers and then select how you respond, particularly when it comes to negative reciprocity. One bad act that you attempt to "repay" or even just one individual complaining about you, directing you to complain about them, forms a helix of negativity that can tangle you down to violent and even horrible places. Most of the world's disputes continue because one group always seeks payback from another and vice versa and to infinity.

Understanding how to control your inner dialogue in reply to negative actions is a perfect way to lay yourself off from reciprocating the same, but that still is not the point I want you to understand. I want you to understand how to make others realize that they owe you one: reciprocity by social influence.

Reciprocity, as explained above, is a manipulative strategy. First of all, it sensitizes one of the multiple things people can do to get you to do their bid. Secondly, reciprocity is an easy technique for those situations where particular endings can vindicate specific means. Reciprocity is handling other people just as they do with you or as you want to be treated – particularly with the prospect that they will reciprocate your favor some other time. Putting it differently, reciprocity is an underhanded trick that allows deliberate interpersonal influence. Be willing to do something good for others, and others will be willing to do something good for you, partly because they will be uneasy in feeling obligated to you.

The idea of reciprocity is deeply rooted in human nature. As part of our raising, we learn to give something in return to people who give something to us. Cooperation and reciprocity are the underpinnings of an educated society that permit us to help people who want it and to expect that they will help us when we require it. Surveys and studies suggest that the urge to repay goodwill is hard-wired in our brains.

Here is an amazing technique to put reciprocity into action. The next time you do good to someone, do not say, "My pleasure" or "you're welcome" rather say, "I know you'd do the same for me". This will invoke reciprocity, and that person is predisposed to give you a favor when needed. The consequences of goodwill are transient.

Moving projects forward in today's blandish organizations, where cross-practicality is the norm, requires the skill to manage ups, downs, and sideways. Line authority and power go only so far. That is where opinion comes in. Much like martial arts fighters overcome their antagonists using inertia, gravity, and leverage rather than crude strength, you can sway others to your side by overworking the principles of reciprocity. These include the sentiments of obligation created between two people when one minimizes their own personal gain, and the propensity to say "yes" to people we like with the expectation to act in ways that are coherent with our values and commitments.

How can you activate reciprocity?

One good reverse generates another. A favor you will do today is probable to be reciprocated down the road.

- Defending a colleague's idea in a meeting when other colleagues are giving it only timorous support.
- Divvying helpful information with a colleague in another part of the enterprise who otherwise would not have gotten it.

- Pitching in to support a teammate with a presentation.

Do not be cold-blooded and do not be insincere. People will know you and be on their safety. Just look for chances to be a good human being. You will not just feel happy, you will make a network of obligated colleagues who will actively find ways to support you and help you out. It is recommended that the favor must be in keeping with the individual's job and will make him look good.

Like reciprocation, concentrating on a person's positive qualities is an ideal procedure to start a relationship. This strategy requires that you endlessly seek for something you like in a person. Even if he is a jerk at work, there might be something you can appreciate about his past experiences, his private interests, and the causes he aids. Once you have discovered the positive qualities, admire him or her on it. By showing him or her your commendation, you help them to compliment you. And that is when the roadblocks come down. People feel more secure, open, and committed to people who like them. They are more likely to give them additional information that will help them build a sense of trust.

Concentrating on the positives can help in bettering relations with colleagues you have historically hated. For instance, a manager at a medical company has a bad relationship with her boss, and the two were mostly at loggerheads. Using this strategy, she realized that his propensity to hold up work was because of his desire to get it done perfectly. When she admired his work on those values, his face brightened. The next morning, he provided her the kind of information he had never divvied before: a comprehensive heads-up on what she should accentuate and be on guard for in hitting buy-in at an important meeting that day.

Without that information, things would not have been so easy. In the way of saying, "I appreciate your top-notch standards", she also provided him a repute to uphold. He realized that if she appeared in a positive gesture, he would too.

Evoke a Person's Old Position

When you prompt someone's old position on an issue, he is more probable to behave in a way that is logical with that position. "Remember, Harry, how you debated that the company should dedicate bigger resources to preparing the sales team about the new product line?" This is a case of the phenomenon recognized as *labeling*. To utilize labeling to impact someone, you are providing him a reputation to uphold. If you expect his support on a proposal to make more marketing cash from print to online ad purchases to drive widget sales, evoke his track record of prioritizing online marketing for items alike to the widget. You expect him to think that supporting your offer is in line with his old positions.

Labeling, as you may think, is specifically effective with someone who highly perceives their own decision-making skill. The strategy needs familiarity with a person's values, preferences, and stated positions. If you have not worked sufficiently with someone to attain his insight, go through the presentation he has given and prudently probe for information about him in conversations with those who are closer to him.

Lastly, influence is all about relationships. The more you have, the securer they are, the better capable you will be to take others to your side when you seek their support.

Let's Honor the Rule of Reciprocation

Here I want to showcase what I consider to be one of the most substantive, yet often unidentified factors built in the practice and art of persuasion and influence. These two extremely important aspects of effective communication are everywhere. Whether it is about business transactions, personal relations, sales, politics, education or any other domain that handles forms of interpersonal transaction, or our skill to influence the point of view of others, these factors are crucial to the accomplishment of our goals and intentions. The two most important aspect are *what's in their head* and *what's in their heart*.

When I mention the head, I am referencing leveraging what makes a person click with your personality traits. What turns the passion on, what motivates them during times of hardship and times of victory? Tapping into a person's head will direct you to the next level which is their heart. Leveraging what's important to any individual starts with trust and proven history of application. I know this sounds simple, but I can assure you that this is powerful to understand. Once you find common ground with someone, it creates a foundation of trust.

Have you ever felt awkward having a conversation with someone new, and once you find common ground it seems like there nothing else to discuss? Most people end the conversation right there and start over with someone else and after the meeting, you are loaded with tons of business cards but no true connections. Here is the key, on your next touch point with a new individual, move past fear to find what's in their heart by sharing something that important to you but relevant to the current situation or event.

Before we end this chapter, I want to be sure we discuss something I feel is important. There is a fundamental difference between "control & command" which has to do with having authority or domain on another and "influence" which has to do with having the talent to affect or sway change in others' views or behaviors. Attempts to control people often result in consequences that dissent from or may even be the inverse of our intended desires. This is because most of us have a natural propensity to protest over the efforts from others to command our beliefs or behaviors.

The "rule of reciprocation" is strongly linked with the universal propensity in human beings to feel obliged to reciprocate or repay when they receive a gift whether it has in the form of a kind deed or the form of a material object or an act of generosity. It is a means of influence, not control.

There is a strong urge in people from different cultures to repay favors or gifts with favors or gifts. This urge expresses itself in reciprocation to requests to parties, birthday gifts, Christmas cards, or acts of kindness. This trend has survived and been portrayed throughout human history because it has endurance value for the human species. We are human because our ascendants learned to share their talent and abilities in an honored network of responsibility.

In every culture, the procedure of socialization trains us to share, take rounds, and give back to all. We are likely to be ostracized or shamed if we do not incorporate the rule of reciprocity into our behavior. Picture this. You are planning a get-together, and you are sending out invitations via mail. You speak to one colleague you have a great relationship with and care for and another colleague who you do not like. You do not honestly want the second colleague to attend your party, but because he invited you to his party last year, you feel obliged, even urged, to invite him to yours.

Let us walk through another scenario. Crazy Aunt Debbie sends you a happy "empty" birthday card. You have not heard from her in a long time. You are not close to your aunt and considering her age, you might never see her again. However, you automatically add her to your birthday wishing list.

You likely encounter scenarios like this many times. You feel indebted, obliged, and duty bound to act a particular way. Why is that? The reason is that you are a human being ruled by human psychology. The principle of reciprocity is the 7th principle of persuasion, which relies on our internal, powerful sense of indebtedness. When someone does good for us, we feel obligated to return it to them. Even if he did that act out of the kindness of his heart, we still feel obliged until we pay it back.

Some experts believe that reciprocity is our brain's mode of simplifying decision-making. As human beings evolved, we developed shortcuts to making fair decisions faster and more reliably. Reciprocity is a shortcut. Rather than using cognitive resources to fix it, we react to another person's actions. Our neurological cabling tells us, "that person did something good for you, now you must do something nice too". Reciprocity can turn your workplace into a more productive and happier place if you know the right way to stir it.

Use a System of Rewards

If you observe an employee exhibiting the behavior you want to promote, reward him without any admonition. Keep in mind, it must be a reward. A nomination for an award, a gift certificate or public acknowledgment for your employee's positive acts at your next employee meeting will go a long way in stirring the rule of reciprocity in your employee. He will be more probable to continue that desired attitude as a thank you for doing something good for him. This is just one way to stimulate reciprocity to improve your workplace, but so many more are usable.

Modern advertisers do this all the time, and you might not even be aware of it. A complete category of marketing, known as content marketing, rotates around this impression of sharing knowledge. In content marketing, advertisers create expert content like articles, blog posts, e-books, podcasts, videos, infographics, webinars, etc. to engage their target audience. Readers and traffic give them exposure. In return they give them high-quality, informative content, and thus, both parties gain profit by following the rule of reciprocity.

By using the following key points, you can positively influence people through reciprocity.

1. Whenever possible, be the first to give something. Be proactive.
2. Whenever it is the time for appreciation, present unique gifts to your employees, and make sure they are given as a surprise.
3. Do not turn into a coy. Let the employee know the reward, resource, or assistance is from you. Reciprocity will not work when the receiver does not know the well-wisher.

CHAPTER 2:
The Key to Strength: Acknowledge Your Weaknesses

One compulsory question that job interviewers regularly ask applicants is a two-part question: First, what are your weaknesses? Second, what are your strengths?

The second portion of that inquiry is not difficult to answer. One is given license to swash a little. The first part of that inquiry is not so easy. If someone interested in employing us knows our flaws, they may make decisions against us. But such reasoning is ridiculous because obviously, we all have areas of flaws! And the amazing thing about that fact is that both our weaknesses and our strengths encourage teamwork, community, and relationship.

Recognizing Weaknesses

To enjoy our strengths, we must first recognize our weaknesses. When we work on a team, it is fun to play off of each other's positive attributes. That means, that I do not have to be responsible for every single thing because God has not endowed me in every field. Sometimes in life, we come to find that the truth is sometimes the opposite of what we believed it to be. For instance, up until the 1960's, pregnant women in the US were recommended to smoke. Not until the 1980's, did people learn that smoking is harmful to the unborn child.

We can name these "facts" as toxic advice. These are pieces of advice we perceive will help us, while in reality, they end up hurting us. When it comes to success, there is a piece of famous toxic advice. I have been told that the only way to success in life is to keep focusing on positive things and keep telling myself that I can get what

I am struggling for, by avoiding my flaws and weaknesses.

It sounds like the perfect thing to do, right?

And yet, the opposite is true. The above advice will make you feel bad about yourself, and it will make it very difficult for you to succeed. To be fantastic at something, we have to be fearless enough to look at what we can improve. We need to recognize and accept our weaknesses. Many people believe that being strong means covering any weakness or anything that could be thought of as weakness from other people. Often, perfectionists attempt to hide their flaws from even themselves. This is counterproductive. In reality, the strongest people are those who recognize their weaknesses and use that knowledge to help themselves and others.

Acknowledging Weaknesses Makes You Responsible

Whenever you identify something that you are not specifically proud of, you allow yourself to be more responsible. It is out of the question for you to deal with your weaknesses if you deny recognizing that they are there. Furthermore, when you refuse to acknowledge that a habit, emotion, or problem exists, it is inclined to come up at awkward times, causing you to feel out of control and powerless. Conversely, if you recognize that a weakness subsists, you can avoid putting yourself in a situation when you can enact that weakness. You also will have more hold over your demeanor in all situations.

For example, imagine you have a propensity to drink too much on the weekends. If you are guilty of this imagined weakness and try to pretend it does not exit, you will find yourself going to weekend parties where there is a lot of alcoholic beverages available and end up drinking too much. This will cause more guilt and embarrassment, which can cause you to try to ignore your weakness even more. Rather, if **you** recognize that this is your weakness, you can decide whether or not to go to parties that involve alcohol and come up with plans to avoid it if you still want to go.

Turn Your Imperfections into Perfections

Once you identify your weaknesses, you can change them into strengths. This is particularly encouraging if you have skills that you believe to be weaknesses in the job or in life in general. Think about this for a moment, there is a great statement that says people fail because of what they don't know. I have had many coaches in my life that only wanted to focus on their strengths and ignore their weakness. Not understanding or being aware of your weakness can prevent you from recognizing the right people to help you scale your ideas from a dream to reality.

For example, some people's management and organizational expertise are weak. If you realize yourself that you are not very organized, you can choose to see it from a different perspective: you are probably flexible and spontaneous and able to change your routine easily to re-prioritize.

While concentrating on these strengths, obviously, it is substantive to also work on your imperfections so that they do not become liabilities. You will want to make an organizational system for yourself that you can survive with, so you can find papers as required and get work done in a well-timed manner while staying flexible. Or you can simply hire or develop someone to do this for you.

Increases Your Self-Esteem

Whenever you deny accepting some attribute about yourself, it damages your self-esteem. After all, your weaknesses are an important part of what makes you, you. One of the easiest ways to enhance your self-esteem is to calmly acknowledge your weaknesses. For example, if you never get to places on time, instead of blaming yourself when you are late again, take a deep breath, relax, smile and say to yourself, "Today, I'll be there on time". With practice, you can acknowledge your weaknesses and can learn to cope with them. It will surely help in boosting your self-confidence.

For all these reasons, it is substantive to identify weaknesses rather than refusing to acknowledge their existence. As nobody is perfect, there is no reason to expect you to be perfect. If you genuinely do not like a specific weakness, you can always work on improving yourself, but before you can do that, you first need to recognize your weaknesses.

Different is Not Bad; It is Just Dissimilar!

When we have a deficiency of understanding ourselves and others, it can lead to real problems such as disappointment, tension, unmet expectations, poor communication, and hurt feelings. As you know, it is difficult to work with issues, specifically if you do not know what is going on secretly inside the mind of another person.

One Simple Procedure to Understand People!

The good news is that there is a simple way to understand how people react and behave and how they are encouraged and inspired. The concept is called "The DISC Model of Human Behavior". This model will permit you to unlock the enigma behind developing good people qualities and creating improved relationships. You will be able to use what you study in this introduction to minimize conflict, improve productivity, and link up with others more efficiently.

Disc Personality Skills

DISC is a quadrant model of behavior based on the research done by Dr. William Moulton Marston to analyze the behavior of individuals in their circle or within a particular situation. It thus focuses on the preferences and styles of such behavior.

The DISC theory is mostly visualized as a quadrant where the top/bottom or right/left sides exemplify particular behavioral tendencies.

People who rank high in dominance and compliance are inclined to be more task oriented. Likewise, people who rank higher in influence and steadiness are usually more active and assertive. Those who rank higher grades in compliance and steadiness enhance calmness and more careful behavioral styles.

A Brief History of the DISC Model

Thousands of years ago, philosophers and scientists, even all the way back to Hippocrates, started to identify and classify differences in behaviors that appeared to follow a pattern. Since then, many more scientists and psychologists have discovered behavioral patterns. In 1928, Dr. William Moulton Marston published "The Emotions of Normal People" after receiving his doctorate from Harvard University. Marston hypothesized that people are encouraged by four intrinsic forces that lead to behavioral patterns. He used four descriptive features for behavioral trends which are symbolized by four letters: D, I, S and C. Hence, the concept of "DISC" was born.

Skills or Dimensions

There are four basic personality skills or dimensions within the disc model. These skills are dominance, influence, steadiness, and compliance.

D – DOMINANCE

Expresses the way you deal with the ups and downs, how you control situations, and assert yourself.

I – INFLUENCE

Expresses the way you deal, relate, and communicate with others.

S – STEADINESS

Expresses your temperament, persistence, patience, and thoughtfulness.

C – COMPLIANCE

Expresses how you access and organize your actions, procedures, and responsibilities.

How Can You Understand a Person by Using DISC?

Every person in this world has a built-in perspective of who he or she is. Some people call it personality, some call it a temperament. Have you ever observed how different your friends and family are compared to you? If you are like me, have you ever asked yourself, why did I do that? Or what was I thinking? The initial step to recognize people is identifying and accepting one simple truth: Everybody is different!

Have you ever experienced two completely different reactions to saying the same thing to two different people? How can saying the same thing create such different results? Every person hears you differently based on his or her personality style. You said the same thing, but what they heard was different.

Ramping Up on a "Wellness" Model

Many behavioral models concentrate on what is missing in a person to recognize "personality disorder". The DISC model is grounded on normal behavior and not on abnormal behavior.

DISC is a wellness model that is descriptive and objective rather than judgmental and subjective.

A Positive Approach

The DISC wellness framework is a good model for understanding people. Healthy, strong relationships come from having precise appreciation of yourself and others. DISC is a potent tool for understanding our personality styles and their consequence on our everyday lives. We use this model with four basic personality traits (DISC) that permit this skill to be used fittingly as an encouraging and effective tool. Your strengths should persuade you while your blind-spots should relate you. Being able to recognize and articulate your strengths can be very empowering, likewise, so can being able to uncover and identify blind spots. The DISC model of a human being is grounded on two basic observations about how people usually behave.

Observation 1: Some people are reserved while others are outgoing.

You can consider this skill as every person's "pace" or "internal motor". Some people always look ready to "drive in" and "go" speedily. They pursue their motor rapidly. Others incline to engage their motor more cautiously or slowly.

Observation 2: Some people are more people-oriented while others are more task-oriented.

You can consider this as every person's "external direction" or "preference" that leads them. Some people are centered on getting things accomplished; others are more tuned to the people around them and their feelings.

With both observations, I want to highlight that these behavioral propensities are neither right nor wrong; they are just dissimilar. We are simply recognizing normal behavioral styles. People have different styles, and that is fine.

Every person has their own set of beliefs, values, and perspectives. We may not always understand what is happening in their minds, but there are tools that can help us make extremely irritating interactions easier. It comes down to understanding and applying empathy in your daily behavior. Empathy is the skill to understand and share another person's emotions. To use empathy is to be able to visualize another point of view reliably.

Why the DISC Model?

The DISC model teaches empathy. The DISC personality judgment is the ideal source for a person to understand how to adjust their behavior to the situation. This is the reason the DISC model is used over other like-minded tests such as The Color Code, Myers-Briggs, or the available myriad of options. The Myers-Briggs test gives a casual understanding of how a person works without giving particular information or advice. That is a vital lesson to learn for understanding and self-growth, but it does not describe how you will respond and act in different situations. The DISC model provides a more adaptive flexible assessment and tools to communicate and understand more effectively as you go about your hectic, busy life.

To use empathy is to be able to focus on another perspective reliably. The more you study the different types, the better you can understand how to stay approachable and how to be more self-asserting.

As mentioned previously, the four major personality skills discussed in the DISC model are dominance, influence, steadiness, and compliance. We will cover each of these in more detail now.

D-PERSONALITY: Dominance

General Behavior

A person with D-personality is probably assertive, decisive, independent, and direct. They are vivid competitors that prosper with ambitious targets and challenges, prioritizing actions over analysis when they need to finish a task. D's are also comfortable with conflicts and may push tougher than other more peaceful personality styles to put forward their will and handle a situation.

Temperament

A D-personality will normally speak confidently but will also be quick to end a conversation they consider pointless. Their ideas will be opinionated, blunt, and high-level, but you normally will have no issue understanding where they stand on a problematic situation. D's are less probable to want to ease into a situation. Rather, their take-charge behavior directs them to zoom in, often before evaluating the whole scenario. Look out for a D on a delegation. Once the target is in view, there is little that can stop them. Still, they are open to external perspective, if they think it will help in the completion of the task.

Briefly, D's are highly competitive individuals and prioritize leadership roles.

How Can You Identify a D-Personality?

These are the four terms which can be used to recognize a D:

- Pushy
- Decisive
- Adventurous

- Competitive

Their Way of Communication

As in action, a person with a D-personality will communicate in the best way. Clipped, short statements are D's casual way of responding or giving instructions. A D-personality visualizes the world in wide terms and prefers, even asks, to omit the details. Do not think about making small talk with a D-person. From their point of view, light banter is just a waste of time and does not direct the conversation towards any action.

Main Qualities of the D-Personality

1. D's are so centered on achievements that most communication will concentrate on results and not on methods.

2. D's will mostly overlook strategy and logic, rather prioritizing to find out the solution as they go.

3. D's are highly objective people. They do not make conclusions based on feelings and sentiments.

4. D's movements are extremely fast, and they enjoy physical activities/games.

I-PERSONALITY: Influence

General Behavior

People who are recognized as I-personality like fun. They are full of energy, confident, engaging, and highly approachable people. These individuals enjoy social settings, and they value linking up with others. They are always trying to enhance their network and social circles by spending time with friends, old and new. They get emotional to explore new ideas and start new projects and are likely to bounce around on what they are working on. I's prefer to multi-task and be in on multiple things at once. I-personalities are cozy people, they are emotional and welcoming, and they have a genuine interest in the feelings of other people. Their social awareness and openness are perceived charming to those who act with them.

Temperament

The trust and authority of an I-personality exhibit is very evident. They are talkative and outgoing and incline to act positively in whatever situation they catch themselves in. They are extraneous processors, which means they plan loudly and may share their ideas and feelings very candidly. I's hold incredible communication skills. That instinctive ability, combined with their concentration on the people around them, makes them outstanding leaders. The perfect way to recognize an I-personality is to observe them walking into a room. They will meet and greet everyone without hesitation before taking their seat or nailing down a conversation.

How Can You Identify an I-Personality?

These are the four key terms to recognize an I-person:

- Inclusive
- Talkative
- Outgoing
- Creative

Their Way of Communication

I-personalities are very talkative about anything and everything. They are blunt and expressive and will mostly gesture with their hands and use facial expressions to communicate a message. Spare lots of time for social conversation, even in a professional environment, when you are surrounded by an I-personality. I's enjoy brainstorming and getting together but will hesitate making major decisions on the spot. However, they are naturally sharp and keen. They are visual people who like to go through everything that was highlighted and discussed.

Main Qualities of the I-Personality

1. I's work very hard to keep a positive environment.
2. I's will use their forever charisma and communication skills to convince others, particularly in terms of viewing their perspective.
3. I's prosper on approval and are encouraged by public admiration.

4. I's enjoy new projects and brainstorming and can have the propensity to take on too much fast.

S-PERSONALITY: Steadiness

General Behavior

S-personalities are normally shy people who search for consistent, like-minded loyal, and supportive individuals in their relationships. They are famous for being openhearted to others' points of view as well as good listening skills. This leads to the steady calm environment and situations they might look for intentionally. This steady skill makes the S's incredible in situations that demand diplomatic skills and assessment of character. Although an S-personality might wait for the other person to start a relationship, they are very reliable for maintaining relationships once they have been grounded. That being said, their circles of friends are usually small and highly tight knit. S's are strongly loyal and will work hard to maintain relationships with their close ones and try their best to make them valued.

Temperament

S-personalities are comfy people who use intention in all of their statements and actions. They are kind and patient in their replies and are quite serious-minded in all that they do. S's are gentle by nature and can be open to strangers and new surroundings but take time to judge the situation and adapt it. Their shy nature can mostly be misunderstood as cold, something S's try hard to overcome. S-personalities like to work endlessly, without any interruption and will firmly resist conflict and change.

S-personalities balance out the more extroverted types and back up those that are more analytical. They are the supporters among all the four personalities.

How Can You Identify a S-Personality?

These are the main words that can help you identify a S-personality:

- Mediator
- Patient
- Methodical

- Reassuring

Their Way of Communication

S-personalities are mostly soft-spoken. Their reserved nature is often misinterpreted as pristine or formal, particularly in writing. It is important not to overwhelm or come on too casual in the first couple of meetings with an S-personality. Rather, S's prioritize creating warmth and trust through more purposeful conversation. This is essential to note while working with a S-personality. The more efficient types may neglect the need for small talk and personal anecdotes and head right to the crux of a problem, but S's thrive on these small talks.

Main Qualities of the S-Personality

1. S's are highly respectful of their colleague's space and will very seldom interrupt anyone to assert their thoughts or opinions.
2. S's like to strategize.
3. S's are motivated and stirred by structured routine and stability.

C-PERSONALITY: Compliance

General Behavior

C-personalities are very analytical and move towards process, rules, and structure. C's are extremely skeptical and use logic to make decisions with objectivity, rather than being persuaded by emotions. If the data introduces new logic, a C-personality is capable of being pliable and changing their minds fast. C's are mostly inventors and need accurate, innovative solutions to the exciting new projects with their problems they are entrusted to.

Temperament

C-personalities are autonomous and reserved people who generally prefer to work independently for a long time of focused work instead of multi-tasking. While they love thoughtful, long conversations about difficult subjects, a C-personality is usually marked by stoic, steady demeanor which can look robotic at times. C's mostly make links with the people around them by detecting common interests that can be discussed in-depth and in detailed discussions. They very seldom offer personal anecdotes impulsively.

How Can You Identify a C-Personality?

These are the four key terms to recognize a C-personality:

- Purposeful
- Analytical
- Accurate
- Structured

Their Way of Communication

C-personalities are very objective and might not utilize much modulation in their natural speech. They can appear dry and distant until motivated by a like-minded idea or interest. They enjoy thorough, long analysis but will neglect small talk because it mostly makes them uneasy. Because of the quantity of time a C-personality spends evaluating details, they can often appear pessimistic. This is not inevitably true, but to a C-personality, the truth is the truth. It is difficult to argue with this kind of data-driven logic.

Main Qualities of the C-Personality

1. C's will employ analytical logic and facts to describe almost every situation in their lives.

2. C's are our "facts and figures" personalities.

3. C's are marvelous at forming and enforcing rules. They can be counted on to neglect distractions and stay grounded.

4. C's are majorly encouraged by proving themselves to be correct by data.

Learning this skill will take more than reading and then applying, but once you have learned and utilized this tool, you will have access to build long-term relationships that are dependable. Learning this skill has been one of the shifts that created momentum in my career and business. We, at the Think My Way to the Top Community, offer several modules that can help you learn this skill and embrace the confidence in new conversations.

CHAPTER 3:
Work before Raise

Psychologists say that the fear of rejection is one of our most cryptic fears. Without a doubt, many of us can recall a time in our careers and lives when we have received rejection, whether it was applying for a new job or asking someone out on a date. But there is something even more spine-chilling than rejection in a new relationship – it is being rejected when you are already attached to someone. Being dumped by a close person hurts more than rejection on a dance floor. And being dismissed hurts more than not being employed in the first place.

In the past few decades, the market has made layoffs a common theme that has resulted in the remaining employees taking on extra responsibilities, often without extra pay. Now that the market is showing signs of improvement, I expect these workers will be bolder about demanding help or demanding more salary at least.

How Soon Can You Ask for a Raise?

We all want to earn more at our jobs, and sometimes, coming out and demanding a salary increase is the only path to get there. By the way, only 37% of employees have asked their current employer for an increment according to payscale.com. Many apparently believe the historical statement that you should not ask for more money because it is associated with greed (which is not the case).

However, there is a good time and a bad time to demand a raise and jumping the gun could lead the conversation to go poorly. The question is: how soon is too soon to request a salary raise?

The One Year Rule Does Not Always Apply

Normally you should wait until you have been at your job at least a year before demanding more money. The upside of waiting is that by then, you will have set yourself up as an appreciated employee who has gained the right to make that request. The negative aspect of this is losing out on currency you could use right away.

There are multiple scenarios where it absolutely pays to inquire for an increment well before the one-year mark. For instance, if you have earned your company more than your salary, you have every right to sit down with your manager and demand to be salaried accordingly. If your responsibilities have enhanced drastically (even without a title change), there's nothing wrong with planning a conversation with your boss and requesting that your salary reflect the degree of effort you are putting in.

It is often the case that workers are hired to do one thing but end up doing far more than they were hired to do. If that's the situation, then you're more than warranted in having that increment conversation several months in, or whenever you come to understand that the job you're doing is much more difficult and time-consuming than the job description showed it would be.

If you have been at the same job for several months, and you're doing the same thing now that you were doing when you first started, then you might have a tough time successfully getting a raise. However, that does not mean you cannot request one, specifically if you research and discover that you are earning substantially less than the average worker with this job title.

Questions to Ask Yourself Before Asking for a Raise

Before planning to demand a raise, make sure you have poised yourself as powerfully as possible for a yes by asking yourself these questions.

1. **How long have you been in this company?**

As mentioned before, normally you should be in a job for at least one year before demanding a raise. Exclusions to this are if the job shifted dramatically or if your responsibilities have risen far beyond what was projected when you were initially employed. In a situation like that, it could be fair to question your recompenses, but in most circumstances, you should wait until you have been employed for a year.

2. **When did you have your last raise?**

Once again, the answer is the same: one year. Generally, it is sensible to ask for your pay to be reviewed yearly, so if you got an increment six months ago, you possibly have another six months to wait before you can fairly demand another one. (Obviously, the exclusions above apply here too.)

3. **How has your worth to the company enhanced?**

An increment is an acknowledgment that your worth to the company has enhanced; it is a recognition that you are producing at a prominently higher level than when your pay was last determined and that you should be salaried accordingly. An obliging argument for an increment should be worked up around that question: not around your heightened expenses, or the fact that a year has gone by or anything else not associated to the worth of your work. And you are speaking of the worth of your work.

4. **Do you know what the current market value is for your work?**

Knowing the market value of your work, signifying what companies similar to yours are paying in your geographic area, is one of the most essential things for you to know. It will prescribe what size increment you can reasonably demand, as well as whether you will be in touch with market curves or unrealistic about what you could make if you moved somewhere else. The better sense you have of the running rate for your work, increases your success of your request.

5. **Are you surpassing expectations or just meeting them?**

Your opportunities increase the more your manager assesses your work. If you are just getting by and meeting expectations but not going over and beyond, a cost-of-living adjustment to your pay might be the most you can wish for. But if you are in the top level of performers on your team, your manager is more likely to go to bat for you to get you a reasonable increase. They will be highly encouraged to do what they can to keep you and ensure you do not jump the boat.

6. **Is this a good time to ask for a raise?**

If the company is laying-off your colleagues or otherwise in a crude financial period, they are probably searching for places to reduce costs, not increase them. You do not want to appear unaware of those challenges, plus, organizations often suspend salaries during hard financial times.

7. **Do you know what you will say if your manager said no?**

Hopefully, when you ask for an increment, you will get a positive response. But you might get refused, and you do not want to be caught unprepared if that happens. Work out what you will say in that situation so that you are not put on the spot. For example, you might inquire what you would need to do to get a raise in the future and what a suitable period for that would look like. Whether or not you are satisfied with that answer, you will be fortunate for being fortified with that information.

Steps to Ask for a Raise

Before you demand a raise, pursue these steps to enhance your chances of actually receiving it.

1. **Frame your case.**

It is not sufficient to simply want the raise or think you deserve it. Can you frame a strong case as to why your salary must be increased? Is it that you are paid too little compared to the market? Is it that you are an above average employee and are contributing more than is reflected in your salary? What are the particular business grounds why your employer should raise your salary right now?

2. **Accumulate market data.**

If contenders are paying more for the same duties, then you have a solid case to present to your employer. If they are not willing to give you a raise, they risk losing you and other above average performers to the broader market. If the market data does not endorse your case, it is still substantive that you know this before you demand a raise. You still must form your argument around other compelling reasons why you should still get your incremental increase despite the market data.

3. **Accumulate personal performance data.**

If you are a high performer who is importantly contributing to the bottom line, then this also provides you a good reason for getting a raise. Get proof of your part. Save emails of admiration and appreciation from colleagues. Detail the particulars for customers who only want to deal with you, or sales that were originated by your ideas or projects that you have had a hand in taking to success. Detail cost savings or streamlined procedures or anything else you believe will help you calculate your bottom-line impact. Do not ever think that your boss knows your achievements, particularly since duties have changed in this volatile market.

4. **Research potential objections.**

What are the possible protests your boss will have to your salary increase request? It could be that your boss understands the market pays more and that he or she admires and values your part, but there currently is not room in the budget, or increments are never allowed this time of year. Research any and all possible objections you think your boss may invoke and come up with answers in advance. In the best case, you want to schedule your request before funds have been decided for that time period.

5. **Look for other positive upshots.**

More money in hand might be the goal, but would you be willing to accept a one-time bonus rather than an increase in salary? How do you feel about equity or variable bonuses? Is extra time off or tuition compensation or another perk just as valuable to you? You do not want to limit yourself to only have one final result in mind because then your request becomes a yes/no issue rather than a dialogue where genuine negotiation takes place. But to preclude a yes/no final result, you have to have options to the one thing you are demanding.

6. **Enhance your leverage.**

It is ideal to look for a job when you are in a job. Your present job provides you leverage – you are confident knowing you have one other choice at least, so you do not have to conciliate. You want to have the same benefits while negotiating for a raise. Another offer for more currency is the most definite form of leverage. But anything that gives you assurance to stand by your request is a form of leverage. Some forms of leverage include:

- a savings fund so you know you could leave if you want to,

- an engaged and strong network so you know you can immediately seek another position if you need to,

- a valuable and diverse skillset so you know you would be suitable to other employers

The Proper Way to Demand a Raise

If you are going to demand a raise before you have been on the job for one year, you should have a strong argument, genuine data, and a target in mind. For instance, if you have been at your job for 30 weeks and have delivered your services on time almost every night for 25+ of those weeks, that is a genuine reason to demand more money. Be sure to bring along a report showing what kinds of tasks and work hours you have logged, so your boss can see for himself. Likewise, if you are going to ask for a raise based on your genuine job being very dissimilar than its original description, find the original document and get it in front of your boss.

When you go in for this conversation: be direct. Do not tiptoe around the issue. Start the conversation with, "I understand I haven't been here for a full year yet, but...". Go straight to the point. In this way, your boss is less likely to fixate on the fact that you are demanding more money after a comparatively short time frame. That said, be ready for the chance that your manager will not be inclined to talk about a salary raise until the one-year limit is reached. If that is the situation, you will need to be patient, but it does not hurt to try.

Choosing the right time to demand a raise is the key to getting it. When deciding the right time, find out when your organization's fiscal budget planning happens, so you can make sure that you are not asking for a thing that is very difficult.

Some of the Best Times to Demand a Raise

- Annual performance reviews

An obvious time for this conversation may be at your annual performance review when the salary raise is often expected.

- After completion of an important project

After the successful completion of an important project or exhibiting excellent work, you can ask for a raise.

- When your boss is happy

Demanding a raise during a hectic or stressful period will assure that your boss is short on time and patience. Be patient to demand a raise until the matter is settled, and you have, once again, proven yourself.

What Should You Say to Get a Raise?

After gathering your evidence for why you are worthy of a raise and choosing a good time to talk to your boss, it is vital to think about what you will say during this conversation. You do not need to have a hard-and-fast script, but you need to be specific and clear in your delivery.

Be Transparent

A simple way to start a raise discussion is to say something like, "As I'm looking forward to working and grow with the organization, I want to discuss my pay".

Be Particular

Mention your expected salary number and particularly highlight how you came to this result.

Bring a copy of your known value salary evaluation. Also, be very clear about when you would like your new expected salary to be effective and any other details that are to the point of your desired recompense.

At the time of this writing, we are 4-5 months into the COVID-19 pandemic. The job market is dramatic, with unemployment at an all-time high in almost 50 years. Employee retention has also plummeted, with voluntary resignations rising more than 60% between 2016-2019, according to the latest research by the Bureau of Labor statistics. Hiring companies are scrambling to tack on to top talent. It takes some practical judgment to demand a raise – even in the ideal times. If you do not get the desired answer, follow up, and demand a raise later.

Play the Conversation out Before

Do not let the first time you are demanding a raise be the real meeting with your boss. You want to rehearse making the request, combatting the objections, answering questions, and sharing your data. You want to feel your nervousness and know you can break through anyway. You need to practice the dialogue, so you can practice on unexpected questions and learn how to better your response. Work with a trainer, a mentor, or someone who can give you a feeling of the genuine event **before** it occurs.

You very well might deserve an increment. But just because it is fair and right does not mean it is going to occur. You have to inquire, and you will have to do so in a convincing manner. So, before you submit a request in that meeting, go through your strategy and merge the steps above.

CHAPTER 4:
Know the Language

Some think of it as English or Mandarin. Others say it is the elusive, culture-spanning hints picked up by reading physical movements and facial expressions. But most people agree that the true language we must understand to make our value in a particular arena is the language of business. The story of any industry, no matter the size, the company, or the country of origin, is spoken through its financial reports and records. As the standards of what you can and cannot say in a business situation are more liberal today than they used to be, rules of thumb still exist for using a proper business language, regardless to what is going on.

Listen carefully to those around you in the office meeting or business situations. Make assessments of the people you come in contact with, try to learn how they speak, what they say, and how it is received. Ask a direct person to criticize your speaking, grammar, vocabulary, voice, and your speaking style. You may receive an eye-opener about the way others think of you.

Try your best to eliminate slang from your vocabulary. Even slang that is widely used within an industry may not be taken well by people outside of the industry. Examine the basic rules of grammar. Begin by always using full sentences and ending sentences with words other than phrases. Read books, purchase audiobooks, attend seminars on the topic of conveying your message effectively, amending your speaking voice, or enhancing your vocabulary to get you commenced.

Seminars and audiobooks are specifically effective because they permit us the opportunity to hear an expert on the subject. Do not forget your manners. "Thank you" and "please" are often neglected in today's busyness, but in the business world, these simple social graces tell volumes about you. Keep your temper in control. This will help in avoiding the situations in which you have stated something you cannot undo.

Pay close attention to the kind of people in your circle. Jokes and memes about the pope might not hurt you if you are a Baptist, but possibilities are the Catholics in your group will not enjoy the humor. So be very careful of your surroundings.

Use a voice recorder to work on getting rid of a strong accent, amending the strength and quality of your voice and to notice pronunciation mistakes you may not even know you are making. Playing back the voice recorder is a good way to supervise your progress during this self-betterment project.

A Word of Advice

Never use derogatory words, demeaning phrases, sexist phrases, and profanity. Ignore stereotypes whenever you can. Do not expose too much information about your personal life or the personal lives of others in your work groups.

What is the Language Etiquette?

Establishing and maintaining a professional repute is substantive in dealing with co-workers, clients, and potential customers. Whether you are talking face-to-face, over the phone, or via email, always use professional language and a tactful method of communication. While email, phone, or face-to-face conversations have their own particular etiquette rules, in every scenario, good manners can go a long way.

Give an Impressive Introduction

When you call someone, dial into a phone/online conference, or are connecting to new people, properly introduce yourself. Say your name, your role, and if the situation requires, your position in the company or business. If you are meeting someone personally, give a solid handshake, and reiterate their names in your head. Saying their names will be helpful for you to remember them in the future.

Use Titles

Not everyone in your office wants or needs to be addressed by official titles like Mr. or Mrs. When people introduce themselves to you, they are telling you how they wish to be addressed by you. If you are naming someone who has a higher rank in the company or he is a client, address them with an appropriate title.

Use Proper Grammar

When speaking or writing, follow grammatical rules. Use complete sentences, proper capitalization, and spell check while sending emails. Use exclamation points sparingly (and really only when necessary). Emoticons and slang do not belong in professional places.

Use a Professional Tone

Do not insult your co-workers or management, berate your employees, or use profanity in the office. The workplace is not the right place to casually release your work-related grudges. Personal emails can easily be forwarded to unintentional parties, and personal conversations may be taken out of context or used against you, resulting in embarrassment or possible sanctions from your employer. Even if you are friends with your co-workers, limit workplace chatter to work-related issues.

Also, do not talk about sensitive subjects. Private or intimate conversations are not good for the office. Religious beliefs, finances, and politics are off limits; stand back from off-color and crass humor.

You do not have to use a strictly formal tone in all meetings or emails, but constantly remind yourself that the workplace should be professional.

Use Proper Body Language

Be attentive to body language. Maintain good posture and keep eye contact. When you are introducing yourself, look at the person you are speaking to and do not slouch. Be mindful to continually look at the speaker throughout the conversation. Respect their private space. Keep at least a foot between the person you are talking and yourself. Also, do not touch the person you are addressing. You may not mind when someone touches your shoulder or arm, but it can make others feel uneasy.

Email the Subject

When sending emails, explain the subject of the email in the memo line. Readers admire the heads-up on what they are about to read, and they can quickly read important emails if they know the contents. Having a clear and particular subject line will also assist you when the recipient addresses the email later on.

Using a Speakerphone

Inquire before using the speakerphone. Most people want to know if there are others on the phone in addition to you. If it is a one-on-one conversation, do not use the speakerphone. People may think that you are multitasking, and your complete attention is not on the call if you use the speakerphone.

Voicemail Ethics

Practice a professional tone for your voicemail. Keep your outgoing mails/messages professional and straightforward. If you are not near your phone for a lengthy period, explain that you are not in your office and mention your return date. You may also want to confirm an alternative person to contact in your absence. When you need to leave a voicemail, say your name, number, and a short explanation of your call. Always be professional.

Improve Your Language Skills

Professional language skills are essential in this modern era of cut-throat competition and globalization. A worker that has competency in professional language skills is likely to climb up the success ladder with ease. That applies to the entire profession or particular arena as a whole. Companies that can convey their strategies in a precise and clear manner are more probable to reach higher levels of efficiency and profitability. Many employees believe that when a company communicates poorly, resulting from poor language skills, can lead to misunderstanding.

You can improve your professional language skills by using the following ways:

- **Amend your vocabulary**

Increasing your vocabulary is the only key in surmounting the specialized words used in the business language. You can improve your vocabulary by training software that offers a wide range of exercises. Learning commonly used business abbreviations and idioms can increase your vocabulary.

Additionally, you can research the internet to look for the terminology used in the particular field that you are presently employed in. It is imperative that you take on an inquisitive approach and seek the meaning of any business word that you are now unfamiliar with. A business dictionary can prove to be specifically helpful since you will be able to get the complete meanings for new terms and their pertinent usage within business communication.

- **Read business language related material**

You can also increase your vocabulary by reading a variety of material associated with your field or business. Reading current updates and business information will not only permit you to stay abreast with the current modifications in the business environment but also permit you to keep up with any shift in terminology. This knowledge can prove to be necessary when you are communicating with another party or working on client contracts.

- **Watch programs that are business-oriented**

Watching programs that focus on business is a perfect way to gain better language skills because people in those programs frequently (and correctly) use key terms. These programs are usually hosted by experts in that particular arena and thus can prove to be an incredible source of valuable knowledge and information, as well as vocabulary terms. Business terminology is generally used on these programs and watching them with attention can help you grasp terms that are part of professional communications.

Watching or listening to these programs will not only let you become conversant with new words but also learn their right usage and pronunciation. A simple understanding of business terminology cannot entirely wipe out the risk of misunderstanding in organizations; rather, an employee must be able to use the terms correctly so that the underlying message is communicated effectively to the other party. Watching these programs will help you understand the latest business scenarios while also becoming comfortable with a range of words and their perfect uses.

Actions Speak Louder!

"The first impression is the last impression" is a phrase I have heard numerous times. The concept behind this phrase is to emphasize the importance of creating a sound and sweet initial impression on the person you are communicating with.

Studies indicate that when we talk to someone, 60-90% of the communication is not verbal. We observe the sitting/standing style of the person next to us, his way of talking, his stare, and the tone of his voice – just a few factors which speak volumes.

Austrian-American author, Peter F. Drucker frequently says that the most important part of communication is hearing what people aren't saying.

Have you ever had a suspicious feeling about someone you just met, only because his smile was mysterious? We often judge people from the way they behave, and vice versa. If we are talking to anyone, they will also observe our posture, style, and confidence. In the corporate sector, communication is the key to success; and not just verbal communication, the one our body does is more important.

These are a few ways you can adapt to be more confident while communicating and increase your self-worth:

1. Imagine you are having a table talk with your potential client, and you want to present your ideas with grace and style. Being slouchy or sitting stiffly in the chair will not do any good. Do not look too stiff or too relaxed, because the excess of everything is bad. Instead, calm yourself, lean a bit towards the other person, and keep your back firm yet relaxed.

2. Positioning your legs in a formal discussion is always a bit tricky. Some think we should cross the legs, while others prefer keeping them relaxed. To show that you are easy while talking to your client, keep your legs relaxed, slightly crossed, parted or straight.

3. Keeping your arms straight, uncrossed, and comfortable is one of the most preferred gestures of communication. Gesturing too much or too little will not do any good. Maintain a balance and ensure the speaker that you are listening to them.

4. Smiling when the other person says something nice and nodding as a sign of agreement creates a sense of confidence. If you liked what your boss or client said, nod and put a genuine smile on. Smiling excessively could make you look creepy; avoid that.

5. Nodding unnecessarily and constantly staring with no expression is the KILLER of discussions.

6. Maintaining steady eye-contact creates a sense of assurance that you are interested in what the other person is explaining. Additionally, those who can look into the eyes of other person are believed to be confident and challenge-taking people. When communicating, do not look anywhere else, focus on the speaker, and assure them that you understand their concepts.

7. Adding a little humor shows that you are giving value to the listener, which

ultimately strengthens your position during the deal-making process.

8. Be open. Discuss all aspects of the contract with your client and show them that you understand their reservations and expectations.

9. DO NOT interrupt when someone is talking. Let them finish their argument, note down a few bits, and if you have any objections, speak when it is your turn.

10. Leaning forward when there is no need and showing a laid-back attitude when a critical discussion is going on will destroy your reputation in the very first meeting.

11. End the discussion with a confident and firm handshake, escort the person towards the door, and end the session with a positive smile on your face.

Leaving a positive impression on someone is only possible if you learn to maintain balance. TOO MUCH of any gesture can feel weird to the person you are connecting with so be sure not to overuse the gestures during your conversation.

Prove Your Importance

Things are replaceable; in business, so are the people. The business world never settles for so-so performance. If you continue being an average employee, your company will replace you in no time. Many people do not receive the praise they deserve or are compelled to change their jobs simply because they do not know the ways to present themselves. If you want to avoid any nuisance in your corporate career, learning these eight lessons will be imperative for you.

1. **Be consistent.**

Once you achieve a milestone, make sure that you never go below it. Being a consistent worker will earn you recognition, and you will become a valued employee at your company. Whether it is preparing an excellent presentation or meeting deadlines without a fuss, be consistent. Do not let excuses come in your way.

2. **Set high goals; do not be a normalizer.**

No one likes an employee who works like a robot, listens to instructions, and does the job without adding a new aspect to it. Proving your worth at work is a tough job, and you must be ready to take the challenges. If your boss asks you to sell a minimum of 50 products a week, you should keep a target of 60 in your mind. And if you succeed in crossing the set limit, your company will start valuing your efforts, and you just might get a pay raise or promotion.

3. **Never stop learning.**

Let's say you have mastered the skill of persuading your clients through your amazing communication skills. If you stop there, it may not be enough to prove your importance. Learn cold-pitching, cold-calling, and link building. This will add weight to your resume, and you will bring more customers to your company. Keep your routine duties aside and learn new and trending skills. In short, amaze your company with your passion.

4. **Never settle for less than what you deserve.**

If you think that the company is offering less than what you deserve, speak up. Never lower your self-worth thinking that "I might lose my job if I argue" because employers like employees who have confidence. Additionally, if they agree with you, you will get a better offer. So, what is wrong in speaking up?

5. **Arm yourself well when in a corporate battle.**

Businesses are cruel; they will not "understand" if your presentation is incomplete or your arguments are vague. And to stand out from the crowd, you must do your homework before appearing in a meeting/discussion. If you are confident in what you say, your colleagues, seniors, and boss start valuing you. Never lower your guard in the corporate battle; play smart, and ward off all the imminent dangers with logic and facts.

6. **Have confidence in your skillset.**

As I already said, never underestimate yourself. Workplaces are full of competition, envy, and jealousy. To survive in such a harsh environment, you must show a can-do attitude. If you think you might have a hard time in an upcoming task, do not say no. Instead, show interest in learning it, and consult your leaders for guidance. No one knows everything, and if you reject an opportunity for not having prior knowledge about it, your employers will assume you do not have confidence in your skillset.

7. **Do not be a yes man; learn to say no.**

Discussion sessions will raise questions and doubts on your progress, that is something you cannot avoid. But being swayed from those objections will put you in a weak position. You must counter-argue and show that you are well aware of the consequences. If someone is pointlessly harsh, answer them with logic. Simply nodding at every absurd instruction your boss gives you will make you look unprepared.

8. **Take pride in your work; do not let critics surpass you.**

When you achieve something or accomplish a task with positive feedback, cherish it. Whether it was a considerable achievement or a small responsibility, when you have finished, be proud of it. We know critics always like to butt in uselessly and try to belittle your accomplishments.

Always remember, showing your weak points at work is not beneficial. Turn that around: make those weak points learning opportunities for you. Especially when you are working with a company: take responsibility. If the company does well, you are responsible. Likewise, if a company does poorly, you still have accountability.

Do not just be part of the workforce; be a productive part. Learn new skills, hone the existing ones, show enthusiasm in group activities, and take criticism (not the useless kind). When you follow these tips, your company will start valuing you, and new ways of progress will open for you.

CHAPTER 5:
The Law of Attraction vs. the Law of Distraction

The law of attraction is the skill to attract into our life whatever we are concentrating on. It is believed that regardless of nationality, age, or religious beliefs, we are all persuadable to the laws which control the universe, including the law of attraction. It is the law of attraction which employs the power of the mind and interprets whatever is in our mind and makes it a reality.

All thoughts become a reality at the end. If you concentrate on negative doom and gloom, you will keep standing under that cloud. If you concentrate on positivity and have aims that you intend to accomplish, you will find a solution and a process to accomplish it with monolithic action.

This is the reason why the universe is such an immeasurably beautiful place. The law of attraction dictates that the things imagined by the mind's eye are possible if proper plans are made to get there. The law of attraction, just like the law of gravity, is the most energetic law in the universe because its effects are always in motion.

You are always in a state of innovation. You are making your reality every second of your day. You are building the future with every single idea you are having in your mind, whether consciously or subconsciously. As creation is never over, your creativity cannot be stopped. If you want to make changes and make a difference with your existence, expect miracles. Infinite possibilities, endless abundance, and immeasurable joy is permitted by the law of attraction.

What is the Law of Attraction?

The law of attraction is one of the universe's biggest enigmas. Very few of us are entirely aware of how much it impacts our lives. Whether we are following it knowingly or unknowingly, in every second of our life, we are transmitting our emotions and thoughts and attracting back what we have sent out. Alas! So many of us are still blind to the strength that is locked mysteriously within us. Therefore, it is all too convenient to leave our ideas and thoughts unchecked.

This transmits the wrong emotions and thoughts into the universe, thereby attracting undesirable emotions and occasions into our life. It is said that the day you detect the law of attraction in action is a day to celebrate. Once you have realized the power of attraction, it will not be a mystery anymore. You will have found how to efficiently apply these secrets to your daily life and your whole future will be in your hands.

The law of attraction says that whatever you transmit, you will get back more of the same. Whatever you are feeling and thinking at any time, you are requesting the universe to send you the same and more. Positive attracts positive, negative attracts negative. Simply put, if you concentrate on good and positive things in your life, you will automatically attract positivity from the universe.

If you are more focused on negativity and lack in your life, then you will attract that. Because your energy vibes will attract the same frequencies, you must be sure that you are transmitting the feelings, energy, and thoughts that resonate with what you **want** to experience. Thus, if you want more love, more happiness, and more peace in your life, then the vibration frequencies of the same thoughts and feelings are what you must create.

A Short History of the Law of Attraction

Before you set off on the unbelievable journey for true nirvana in the law of attraction, it is crucial that you realize that you can implement it in your life and it can be effectual if the right tools are utilized. The practices and beliefs in this law have been evident in the lives of successful individuals throughout the course of history. Centuries ago, the law of attraction was first believed to have been instructed to a man by the divinity Buddha. It is believed that he coined the idea that "what you have in your life now is what you have desired in your mind". This belief is profoundly intrinsic in the law of attraction.

With the propagation of this concept to Western civilization also came the term "karma", a belief that is famous in several societies. Over hundreds of years, it has been a casual apprehension amongst many that whatever you deliver to the world, you will inevitably get the same or more in your life.

This easy to understand belief has been famous among many for a great number of years. It emphasizes the fact that the concept of the power of attraction is not anything novel. It is already familiar to many of us in multiple ways. The principles of the law of attraction can also be recognized in the teachings of many religious groups and civilizations.

As an illustration, in the Bible, Proverbs 23:7 tells us that a man is as he thinks. Proof of the law of attraction can be seen throughout the ages. It has been taught and recorded in many ways, and yet there for all of humanity to see.

Is the Law of Attraction Genuine?

As explained previously, the law of attraction and its treasures have been experienced throughout history. Many men and women who have left their mark on this universe have depicted the law of attraction to be one of the most amazing powers on earth. Numerous well-loved artists, poets, scientists and thinkers like Blake, Shakespeare, Beethoven, Emerson, and Newton all channeled this message in their main work.

There have been several modern advocates of the law of attraction as well. These include Jim Carrey, Oprah Winfrey, and Denzel Washington. Moreover, with over 6 million social media fans, there are multiple success stories surrounding the law of attraction. The most intriguing acknowledgment of what the law of attraction has to provide is understanding that everything that comes into your life, good or bad, was attracted to you. For many of us, this can be a caustic pill to swallow, particularly if you think that you or your loved ones have experienced some particularly tough challenges in life.

Even then, once you have genuinely come to recognize the key behind the law of attraction, you can be renewed with the courage and hope that you are free to take hold of your life and loose yourself forever from the cycle of worry, fear, and negativity that has restrained you for so long.

The Facts Behind the Law of Attraction

The work of quantum scientists in recent years has drawn attention to the astonishing influence the power of the mind has on us and the universe in general. The more this concept is researched, the greater our understanding is of how substantial a role the mind plays in shaping our lives and the world around us. Whether you have come to a deep understanding of the quantum physics behind the law of attraction or not, you can still experience the countless benefits that this law can provide us.

As physicists provide us with more information regarding this law, we can become more at peace in the knowledge that we are the innovators and controllers of our life. Be glad, for the universe is always supporting us. The more time you spend learning how to use this law efficiently, the more rewarding and satisfactory your life can be. There are no limitations! Open your mind and revel the innate abundance of the universe.

How to Implement the Law of Attraction

Once we realize the astonishing possibilities that life has for us, we can come to understand that we are all creative artists. We are drawing pictures of our desired life and then making selections and taking actions that will draw to us what we imagined. So, what if you do not want that picture? Change it!

Life is a blank canvas of possibilities and opportunities; you can control what the end product looks like. The law of attraction is very simple without any catches. It doesn't matter what you want in your life, if you can make a decision, commit to it, plan and see it for yourself through your mind's eye, you can achieve anything with a little effort on your part. You can decide for responding differently to every situation that happens during the day. You can decide to concentrate and think about the things you want in abundance. You can decide to experience more of the things that make you feel wonderful. You can opt to participate in your future by managing your thoughts and feelings. Using the law of attraction is a three-stage method: inquire, believe, and achieve. Let us have a brief overview of each step.

1. **Inquire: Demand from the universe what you want and do not demand what you do not want.**

Every day, you transmit requests to the universe via your subconscious mind: whatever you talk about, think about, and pay attention to. The law of attraction means that you will get the same or more of what you deliver to the world in energy, attention or focus whether you want it or not. You must become more careful about what you feel and think. To become more deliberate about the thoughts you are sending out to the universe, you must decide what you desire, and rehearse feeling those sentiments that you will feel when you have it. Maybe you want to change location, career, win a professional award, recover from a severe disease, or own a TV channel.

- What would you feel when you finally achieve it?
- What would you do throughout the day?
- With whom will you spend your time?

Focus on what you want to do, and the universe will manifest it for you.

2. **Only Believe.**

What do I mean to believe in your dreams and desires? I am saying that you must maintain a positive expectancy, realizing that you have put your future in the hands of a universe greater than you. You must be convinced in your dreams and desires before the universe can bring them to you. The thoughts, energy, and power you transmit will prompt the universe to deliver to you exactly what you wanted.

Many people are not confident in their beliefs and that keeps happiness and abundance from entering their life. If this keeps you out, understand that you must first change your limiting beliefs into opinions. You must be convinced that you are worthy, capable, deserving, desirable and loveable. Your real work is to convince yourself that you are rich enough, attractive enough, strong enough, and smart enough in every other way that is important to you. Once you trust that you will get what you desire.

3. **Accomplish what you desire by becoming its equivalent.**

To receive that which you were planning for, you must be a strong vibrational match for it. The easiest process to become a vibrational equal is to concentrate on developing positive emotions of joy, love, appreciation, and gratitude all through your day. You should rehearse emotions and feelings you would feel if you already had what you desired. You can also develop these feelings through the plans, ideas, thoughts, and imaginations you have in your mind.

Your emotions are formed by your thoughts all the time. It is crucial to hold yourself accountable when your feelings turn negative and force them to be positive. For everything, it takes time, patience, and practice. The more you practice and put a conscious effort into drawing in what you wish to form, the easier it will turn to be. You can start expecting miracles right now!

The Law of Distraction

The law of distraction is the cousin of the law of attraction. Distraction is linked to the diverting of the focus of a person or group from the selected object of concentration onto the origin of distraction. Distraction originates with one of the following: deficiency to pay attention, deficiency of interest in the object of interest, more interest in something other than the object of interest, more intensity, attractiveness, or novelty of the origin of distraction. Distractions come from both inner and outer sources.

Divided interest is also demonstrated as a distraction in a situation demanding full attention on one object. Interruptions can be linked to distractions because more worth or importance is placed on them rather than the object of interest. The situations that revolve around us greatly influence our life. Every day we make so many choices that are based on our monetary status, past experiences, philosophies, external influences, lack of knowledge, fear, or religious beliefs. We need to defend ourselves against distractions and focus on the things that are important to us. You can practice the following ways to hold against distractions.

1. **Do the important tasks first.**

Try to prioritize things by making a list or plan for everything and follow the rule: first comes first. Start and finish the most important task on your list to avoid distractions.

2. **Build your importunity.**

Make deadlines and try to finish your projects. No one is going to tell you when to set the alarm or when to sleep; you must settle your preferences and take some steps in place to accomplish them.

3. **Set a deadline earlier than the actual deadline.**

Try to always set up your due date at least one day before the actual due date. Finish the project early and watch what happens. Start arranging your due date initially a day in advance and see if you can move that due date up. You will be amazed at how much better you feel when you know your work is accomplished ahead of time.

Tying It All Together

Your mind, thoughts, and beliefs are the most important aspects of bringing your thoughts to reality. As you have completed this book, your journey to the top is just beginning. My life is full of thoughts that have become things and I hope that your thoughts will become things. You may ask what are the next steps? I'm glad you asked.

I have developed a coaching program that will allow you to take the next step to believe and invest in yourself. This book that have you just read, should be read at least once a year. Re-reading it ensures that it would not only become a part of your bookshelf, but it will become a part of your mind. Once it becomes a part of your mind, it will become a part of your actions. And once it becomes a part of your actions, it will become a part of your reality. I encourage you to share this book with others, not only your business colleagues, but with your families and those that you care about the most.

I'll see you at the top!

About the Author

Dr. Adrian Singleton is an activation leader and global speaker with an audience that represents a tapestry of leaders on all scales. He has trained several thousand leaders and led 200 plus kaizen events with over $90 million in savings throughout his career. He is a widely accomplished, versatile, and self-directed senior operations management leader with over 18 years of diverse experience in successfully overseeing all facets of Lean manufacturing, finance, accounting, manufacturing, human resources management, planning inventory control, procurement, quality assurance, safety, and staff management.

Dr. Singleton is keenly focused on rigorous implementation of continuous improvement, productivity optimization, and cost savings initiatives. He also believes in building high-performance teams that respond rapidly to changing priorities in fast-paced environments and with proven problem-solving, negotiation, and decision-making abilities. He also conducts detailed analysis of business challenges to formulate customer-centric solutions in line with business objectives, timelines, and budgets.

To reach Dr. Singleton for coaching, training events, engagements, or other opportunities, contact him at www.bettermesystem.com